...ndship in Islam

...quranic Verses and Sayings from the 14 Ma'soomeen

Islām places great emphasis on friendship, especially having friendships that are rooted in the remembrance and love of Allāh. Since our friends influence us greatly, we should select those people who remind us of Allāh. When we have strong friendships, we are able to build a strong community, which creates a better future for the generations to come.

إِنَّمَا الْمُؤْمِنُونَ إِخْوَةٌ

Surely, believers are brothers (and sisters) to each other.

Sūrah al-Ḥujurāt, Verse 10

It was a very hot day on the battlefield, and the soldiers were defending Islam bravely. After the war ended, I was walking amongst the injured. I saw that one of the soldiers had lost a lot of blood and felt very thirsty, so I rushed to bring him some water.

The fallen soldier held me and said, "Brother, please take this water to the other soldier first. He's more thirsty than I am!"

I did as he said and ran towards the second soldier. However, when I offered it to him, he pointed to the third soldier and weakly said, "He's more thirsty than I am. Give the water to him."

When I reached the third fallen soldier, I saw that he had already become a martyr. So, I rushed back to the second soldier, but he, too, had become a martyr. I then rushed to the first soldier, but by that time, he had also joined his two brothers as a martyr. I was amazed by how they were all so willing to put the needs of others before their own!

Shahīd Muṭahharī, Vol. 17, P. 389

اِلْقَ اَخَاكَ بِوَجْهٍ مُنْبَسِطٍ

Prophet Muhammad (s):
Greet your friends with a smile on your face.

Mizān al-Ḥikmah, #113

وَكُونُوا مَعَ الصَّادِقِينَ

Be with the truthful

Sūrah at-Tawbah, Verse 119

There was once a man who loved Imam Hasan (a) very much, so he asked him, "can I be your friend?"

"Yes, of course. We are already friends," answered the Imam (a).

"But I want to be a close friend, not just any friend," the man insisted.

The Imam (a) looked at him with kindness and replied, "being a close friend has certain conditions. My closest friends should have three traits: (1) they do not praise me falsely, because I know myself better than anyone; (2) they do not lie to me, because lying is bad; and (3) they do not gossip."

The man stayed silent because he knew that he did not meet those conditions. But with hope in his eyes, he told the Imam (a), "O Imam, please give me some time to develop these traits."

The Imam (a) smiled and hugged the man. He comforted the man by telling him that they would soon become the best of friends, inshaAllah, and that his company is always welcome. The man felt ever more inspired to become a better person and try to change his bad habits.

Kalimāt al-Imām al-Ḥusayn (a), P.16

إِيَّاكَ وَ مُصَاحِبَةَ الْكَذَّابِ

Imam Muhammad al-Baqir (a):
Beware of making friends with a liar.

Al-Kāfī, Vol. 2, P. 376

فَأَصْلِحُوا بَيْنَ أَخَوَيْكُمْ

Make peace between your brothers
(and sisters).

Sūrah al-Ḥujarāt, Verse 10

In the time of Imam Sadiq (a), there lived two friends who were so close that they were like brothers. But one day, they got into an argument and stopped talking to each other. When a wise man named Zuraarah noticed that the two men were mad at each other, he decided to invite them to his house. After a long conversation about what went wrong, Zuraarah realized that the two men were disagreeing over money.

"Here," said Zuraarah, "take this money." The two men looked at the money with surprise and confusion.

"Imam Sadiq (a) has told me that whenever two people argue over money, I should give them money on his behalf to help them solve their problem," he explained. "So I'm giving you this money, but only if you go back to being good friends and promise not to argue anymore."

Feeling ashamed, the two men looked at each other and hugged. They thanked Zuraarah and left the house in a good mood.

Usūl al-Kāfī, Vol. 2, Ḥadīth #3-4

صِلْ مَنْ قَطَعَكَ

Prophet Muhammad (s):
If someone breaks their relationship with you,
you should try to fix it.

Tuḥaful ʿŪqūl, P. 305

وَلَا تَنَابَزُوا بِالْأَلْقَابِ

And do not call each other bad names.

Sūrah al-Ḥujurāt, Verse 11

One day, Imam Sajjad (a) was sitting with some of his friends, when a man came up to him and started calling him bad names. The Imam (a) stayed patient and remained silent until the man finished and went home. Seeing this, his friends became enraged!

"How dare he talk to you like that!" exclaimed one friend.

"Why didn't you say anything to him?!" asked another.

The Imam (a) tried to calm them down, but some of them darted out and headed to the man's home. The Imam (a) did not want anyone to bother the rude man, so he said, "follow me. I'll reply to the man myself."

As the Imam (a) made his way to the man's house, he kept repeating a verse from the Quran that talks about holding our anger and forgiving others. Everyone watched anxiously as the Imam (a) knocked at the man's door. They were most curious to see how the Imam (a) was going to deal with the rude man.

When the man came out, he grew scared seeing so many people gathered outside. The Imam (a) kindly greeted the man and gently said, "my brother, if what you said about me is true, then I ask Allah to forgive me. But if what you said about me is not true, then I ask Allah to forgive you."

The man was shocked at the Imam's kindness. With a regretful heart, he kissed the Imam's forehead and said, "The things I said about you were not true!" Hanging his head in shame, he continued, "Those words apply more to me than anyone."
The Imam (a) forgave the man, and they went on to become good friends.

Al-Burhān fī Tafsīr al-Qur'ān, Vol.1, P. 690

تَدْعُوهُ بِأَحَبِّ اَسْمَائِهِ اِلَيْهِ

Prophet Muhammad (s):
Call your friends by their favorite names.

Nahjul Faṣaḥah, #1293

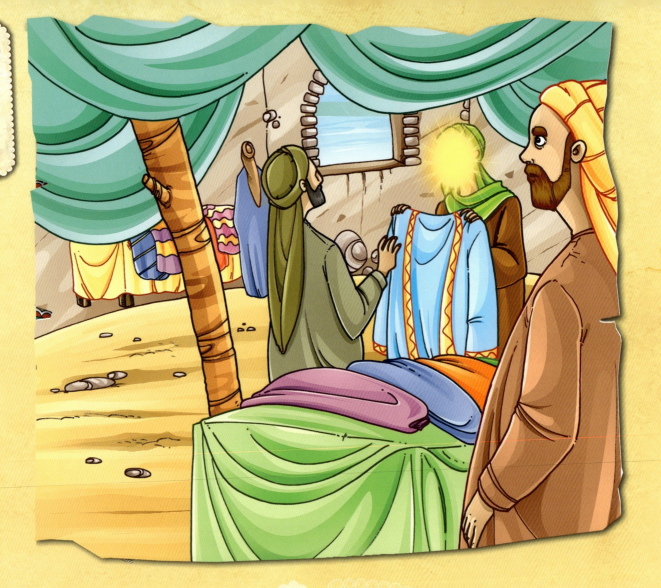

وَ إِذَا حُيِّيتُم بِتَحِيَّةٍ فَحَيُّوا بِأَحْسَنَ مِنْهَآ

And when someone greets you, reply with a better greeting.

Sūrah an-Nisā', Verse 86

It was a day like any other in the marketplace. People were busy buying and selling, and customers were hunting for the best prices. Imam Ali (a) was also shopping with one of his workers, Qambar. He bought two shirts: the first one was very nice, and the second one was very plain.

"Here you go," said the Imam (a) to Qambar as he held out the more expensive shirt. "This is for you, my dear friend."

Qambar was very touched. "O my beloved Imam! How can I take the better shirt? You should wear it!" he pleaded. "You are the one who stands in the masjid and speaks to large crowds of people!"

"But you are a young man, and I would feel embarrassed in front of Allah if I wore better clothes than you," said the Imam (a). He remembered that the Prophet (s) used to say, "give your workers clothes that you would wear, and feed them with food that you would eat."

Biḥār ul-Anwār, Vol. 5

تَهَادُوا تَحَابُّوا

Prophet Muhammad (s):
Exchanging gifts will bring you closer to each other.

Quiz Yourself!

1. Prophet Muhammad (s) tells us to meet our friends with _____.
a. a freshly cooked meal
b. a big hug
c. a smile on our face

2. Imam Hasan (a) said that in order to be his friend, the man should _____.
(Circle all that apply.)
a. not gossip
b. have a good sense of humor
c. not lie

3. Imam Sadiq (a) told his friend that whenever there are two people arguing over money, he should give them money to help them _____.
a. become richer
b. fix their relationship
c. start a business to help the poor

4. How did Imam Sajjad (a) react to the man who said mean things to him?
a. He stayed patient and did not reply.
b. He replied with an ayah from the Quran.
c. He asked the man for an apology.

5. When Imam Ali (a) went with Qambar to the marketplace, he bought _____.
a. two aqeeq rings: one that was blue and another that was red.
b. two shirts: one for Qambar and the cheaper one for him.
c. two loaves of bread: one for his family and one for Qambar.

6. Choose one lesson from this book and explain how applying it in your life can make you a better friend.